Across the Country

18, 19, 20

A Transportation Counting Book

by Martha E. H. Rustad

AMICUS READERS 1 AMICUS INK

amicus readers

Say Hello to Amicus Readers.

You'll find our helpful dog, Amicus, chasing a ball—to let you know the reading level of a book.

1

Learn to Read

High frequency words and close photo-text matches introduce familiar topics and provide ample support for brand new readers.

2

Read Independently

Some repetition is mixed with varied sentence structures and a select amount of new vocabulary words are introduced with text and photo support.

3

Read to Know More

Interesting facts and engaging art and photos give fluent readers fun books both for reading practice and to learn about new topics.

Amicus Readers and Amicus Ink are imprints of Amicus
P.O. Box 1329, Mankato, MN 56002
www.amicuspublishing.us

Library of Congress Cataloging-in-Publication Data
Names: Rustad, Martha E. H. (Martha Elizabeth Hillman), 1975- author.
Title: Across the country 18, 19, 20 : a transportation counting book / by Martha E.H. Rustad.
Description: Mankato, MN : Amicus Readers, 2017. I Series: 1, 2, 3 count with me I Includes index. I Audience: K to grade 3.
Identifiers: LCCN 2015040335 (print) I LCCN 2016000138 (ebook) I ISBN 9781607539193 (library binding) I ISBN 9781681521107 (pbk.) I ISBN 9781681510439 (eBook)
Subjects: LCSH: Counting--Juvenile literature. I Transportation--Juvenile literature.
Classification: LCC QA113 .R888 2017 (print) I LCC QA113 (ebook) I DDC 388.3/4--dc23
LC record available at http://lccn.loc.gov/2015040335

Photo Credits: Corbis/suedhang/cultura, 13; Dreamstime.com/Joggie Botma, 18, 24, Mikael Damkier, cover; Getty/Robert Laberge, 17; iStock/Klaus Hollitzer, 4, muratart, 8, LaserLens, 11, AlbanyPictures, 12, wloven, 14, hanhanpeggy, 15, Marek Mnich, 18, Marcus Lindstrom, 19, AwaylGl, 19, 24, Ridofranz, 20, 24; Shutterstock/turtix, 1, altanaka, 3, Richard A. McGuirk, 5, Irina Fuks, 6, Anna Omelchenko, 7, rCarner, 9, sonya etchison, 10, Cynthia Farmer, 14, Sashkin, 15, Nyvlt-art/21, Monticello, 21, alexdrim, 22, fotoslaz, 23, Balefire, 16, 24

Editor   Rebecca Glaser
Designer   Tracy Myers

Printed in the United States of America

HC 10 9 8 7 6 5 4 3 2 1
PB 10 9 8 7 6 5 4 3 2 1

Let's travel across the
country. Count along!

1

One monorail

glides along

a track.

2

Two airplanes
fly in the sky.

3 Three pedicabs wait for riders.

Four motorcycles speed by.
The riders wear helmets.

5

Five bikes ride up the road.

The riders change gears.

6

Six trucks are loaded onto a trailer.

7 Seven school buses wait for students.

8

Eight people
board a bus.

9

Nine taxis sit in traffic.

10

Ten people wait for a city bus.

Eleven big rocks sit in a dump truck. The bed tilts to dump.

11

12

Twelve loads wait for a crane. Cranes lift loads high.

13

Thirteen hot air balloons
rise into the air.

14

Fourteen race cars speed by. Drivers steer around the track.

15

Fifteen skydivers jump from a plane.

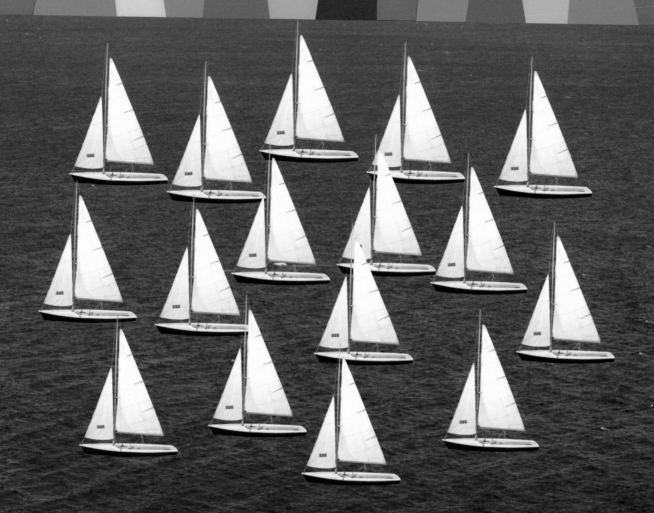

16

Sixteen sailboats sail. Wind pushes them across the sea.

17

Seventeen boxes are loaded

into a moving truck.

18

Eighteen suitcases wait to board a plane.

19

Nineteen windows line this train.
Passengers can see out.

20

Twenty vehicles cross the bridge.

How many can you count?

Count Again

Count the number of objects in each box.

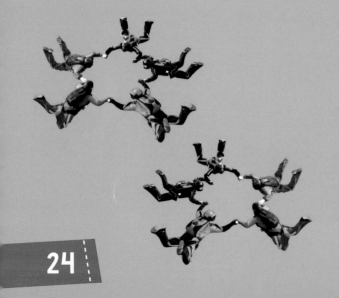

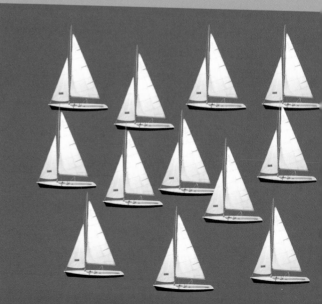